ATLAS of
South
America

by Karen Foster

PICTURE WINDOW BOOKS

First American edition published in 2008 by
Picture Window Books
151 Good Counsel Drive
P.O. Box 669
Mankato, MN 56002-0669
877-845-8392
www.picturewindowbooks.com

Editor: Jill Kalz
Designer: Hilary Wacholz
Page Production: Melissa Kes
Art Director: Nathan Gassman
Associate Managing Editor: Christianne Jones
Cartographer: XNR Productions, Inc. (13, 15, 17, 19)

Editor and Compiler: Karen Foster
Factual Researcher: Joe Josephs
Designers: Fanny Masters & Maia Terry
Picture Researcher: Diana Morris
Illustrators: Rebecca Elliott and Q2 Media
Maps: Geo-Innovations UK

Printed in the United States of America.

Foster, Karen.
Atlas of South America / by Karen Foster. – Minneapolis, MN : Picture Window Books, 2008.
32 p. : col. ill., col. maps ; cm. – (Picture Window Books world atlases).
2-4
2-4.
Includes index and glossary.
ISBN 978-1-4048-3887-1 (library binding)
ISBN 978-1-4048-3895-6 (paperback)
1. Maps-Juvenile literature. 2. South America-Geography-Juvenile literature.
3. South America-Maps for children.
F2208.5

918 REF
DLC

Photo Credits:
Alinari/Topfoto: 9cl; Theo Allofs/Corbis: 20bl; Ricardo Azoury/Corbis: 22tr; Kike Calvo/Image Works/Topfoto: 21t; Carlos
Cazalis/Corbis: 8bl; David Cumming/Eye Ubiquitous/Corbis: 21bl; Fridar Damm/zefa/Corbis: 9b, 22cl; Michael J Doolittle/
ImageWorks/Topfoto: 6t; Silvio Fiore/Topfoto: 18tl; Michael Freeman/Corbis: 27br; Kit Houghton/Corbis: 23cl; David G.
Houser/Corbis: 23bl; Wolfgang Kaehler/Corbis: 29tr; Kurt/Dreamstime: compass rose on 4, 7, 9, 11, 13, 15, 17, 19, 25, 27; Frans
Lanting/Corbis: 10bl; Charles & Josette Lenars/Corbis: 20br; Larry Mangino/Image Works/Topfoto: 24b; Buddy Mays/Corbis:
26cr, 27bl; Boyd Norton/Image Works/Topfoto: 11b; Charles O'Rear/Corbis: 13b; Javier Pierini/Corbis: 6bl; Josef Polleross/
Image Works/Topfoto: 25br; Louie Psihoyos/Corbis: 9tr; Roger-Viollet/Topfoto: 23tr; Galen Rowell/Corbis: 26bl; Albrecht G.
Schafer/Corbis: 8tr; Carlos Silva/Reuters/Corbis: 6br; Hubert Stadler/Corbis: 19b; Steve Starr/Corbis: 24t; Jose Alberto
Tejo/Shutterstock: 18b; Topfoto: 11bl, 23br, 25bl; Peter Turnley for Harpers/Corbis: 20cr; Pablo Corral Vega/Corbis: 22br;
Nevada Wier/Corbis: 28-9; Jan Zuckerman/Corbis: 12t; Picture research: info@picture-research.co.uk

Editor's Note: The maps in this book were created with the Miller projection.

Table of Contents

Welcome to South America. 4

Countries 6

Landforms. 8

Bodies of Water 10

Climate 12

Plants 14

Animals 16

Population. 18

People and Customs 20

Postcard Places 22

Growing and Making. 24

Transportation 26

Journey Around Lake Titicaca 28

South America At-a-Glance. 30

Glossary. 31

Index 32

Welcome to South America

The world is made up of five oceans and seven chunks of land called continents: North America, South America, Antarctica, Europe, Africa, Asia, and Australia. This map shows South America's position in the world.

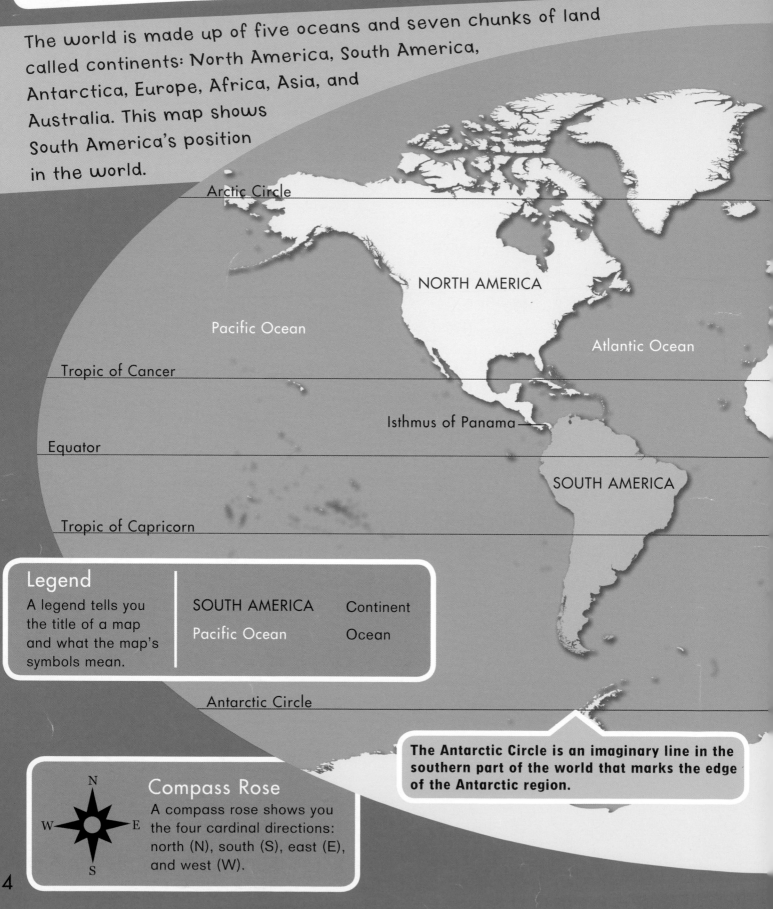

Arctic Circle

NORTH AMERICA

Pacific Ocean

Atlantic Ocean

Tropic of Cancer

Isthmus of Panama

Equator

SOUTH AMERICA

Tropic of Capricorn

Antarctic Circle

Legend
A legend tells you the title of a map and what the map's symbols mean.

| SOUTH AMERICA | Continent |
| Pacific Ocean | Ocean |

The Antarctic Circle is an imaginary line in the southern part of the world that marks the edge of the Antarctic region.

Compass Rose
A compass rose shows you the four cardinal directions: north (N), south (S), east (E), and west (W).

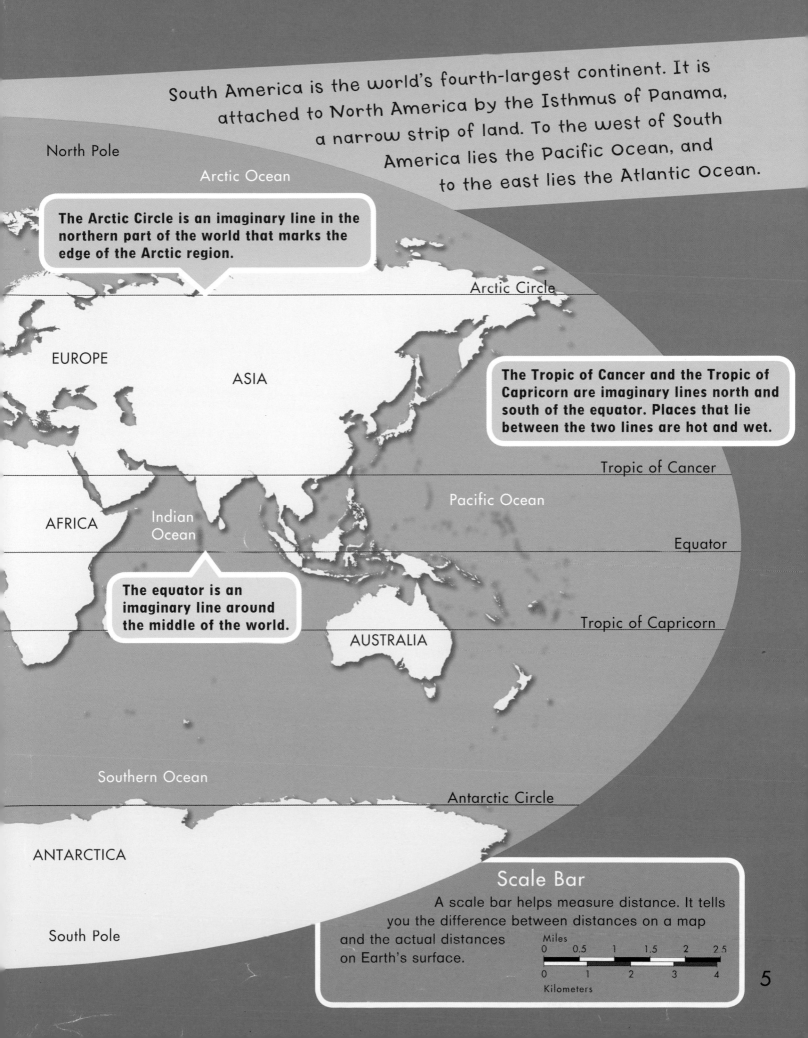

South America is the world's fourth-largest continent. It is attached to North America by the Isthmus of Panama, a narrow strip of land. To the west of South America lies the Pacific Ocean, and to the east lies the Atlantic Ocean.

North Pole

Arctic Ocean

The Arctic Circle is an imaginary line in the northern part of the world that marks the edge of the Arctic region.

Arctic Circle

EUROPE

ASIA

The Tropic of Cancer and the Tropic of Capricorn are imaginary lines north and south of the equator. Places that lie between the two lines are hot and wet.

Tropic of Cancer

Pacific Ocean

AFRICA

Indian Ocean

Equator

The equator is an imaginary line around the middle of the world.

Tropic of Capricorn

AUSTRALIA

Southern Ocean

Antarctic Circle

ANTARCTICA

South Pole

Scale Bar

A scale bar helps measure distance. It tells you the difference between distances on a map and the actual distances on Earth's surface.

Miles
0   0.5   1   1.5   2   2.5

0   1   2   3   4
Kilometers

Countries

South America is divided into 13 countries. The largest is Brazil. The smallest is Suriname.

Most South Americans speak Spanish. However, Portuguese is spoken in Brazil, English is spoken in Guyana, and French is spoken in French Guiana. The official language of Suriname is Dutch.

The Native Americans of South America also have many local languages, such as Quechua, Aymara, and Guaraní.

What's on the menu?

Bolivia – corn husk-wrapped tamales

Chile – seafood stew

Colombia – cinnamon and coconut cream

Ecuador – red pepper and garbanzo bean salad

Paraguay – corn and squash soup

Peru – potatoes with chili sauce

Venezuela – cheese puffs

Let's say "hello!"

Hola
(Spanish)

Oi
(Portuguese)

Salut
(French)

Hallo
(Dutch)

Kamisaraki
(Aymara)

The Native American language spoken by this boy was used long before Europeans brought the Spanish language to the continent.

Time to dance

Many South Americans love to dance. Brazilians, especially, are known for a fast, lively dance called the samba. Samba is the traditional dance of one of Brazil's biggest festivals, *Carnaval*. During Carnaval, thousands of dancers compete in a giant samba contest.

Tango dancers in Argentina

A folk dancer in Bolivia

ARGENTINA

BOLIVIA

BRAZIL

CHILE

COLOMBIA

ECUADOR

FRENCH
GUIANA

VENEZUELA

GUYANA
SURINAME
FRENCH
GUIANA

COLOMBIA

Equator

ECUADOR

PERU

BRAZIL

BOLIVIA

Pacific Ocean

PARAGUAY

CHILE

URUGUAY

Atlantic Ocean

ARGENTINA

N
W E
S

Miles
0   200   400   600   800   1,000

0   400   800   1,200   1,600
Kilometers

GUYANA   PARAGUAY   PERU   SURINAME   URUGUAY   VENEZUELA

Landforms

The land of South America takes many shapes—from mountains to deep canyons and from high, flat plateaus to low-lying plains, islands, and peninsulas.

The peaks of the Andes Mountains stretch down the western side of South America. The highlands in the east are also high and rugged. To the south lie grassy lowlands and higher plains called plateaus. They stretch down to Tierra del Fuego, a group of islands at the continent's tip.

Snow-covered Andes

There are many snow-covered peaks in the Andes. Some are the cones of volcanoes. A volcano is a kind of mountain that can spew out lava, ashes, and hot gases from deep inside the earth. Most of these volcanoes no longer erupt, but some still do.

Gorges

Narrow, steep-sided valleys, called gorges, cut through the Guiana Highlands. The gorges were made by fast-flowing rivers wearing away the highland rock.

A gorge in the Guiana Highlands

Avenue of volcanoes

More than 30 volcanoes form a line, or "avenue," down the middle of Ecuador. One of these, Mount Cotopaxi, is the world's tallest active volcano.

An active volcano darkens the sky over Ecuador.

The highest peak

The highest peak in the Andes is called Aconcagua. Not only is it the highest peak in South America, it is also the highest peak located outside of Asia. Rising 22,834 feet (6,964 meters), Mount Aconcagua lies near the Argentinean/Chilean border.

- The Brazilian Highlands stretch down part of the country's eastern coast.
- The Andes Mountains are the second-highest mountains in the world. The Himalayas, in Asia, are the highest.

8

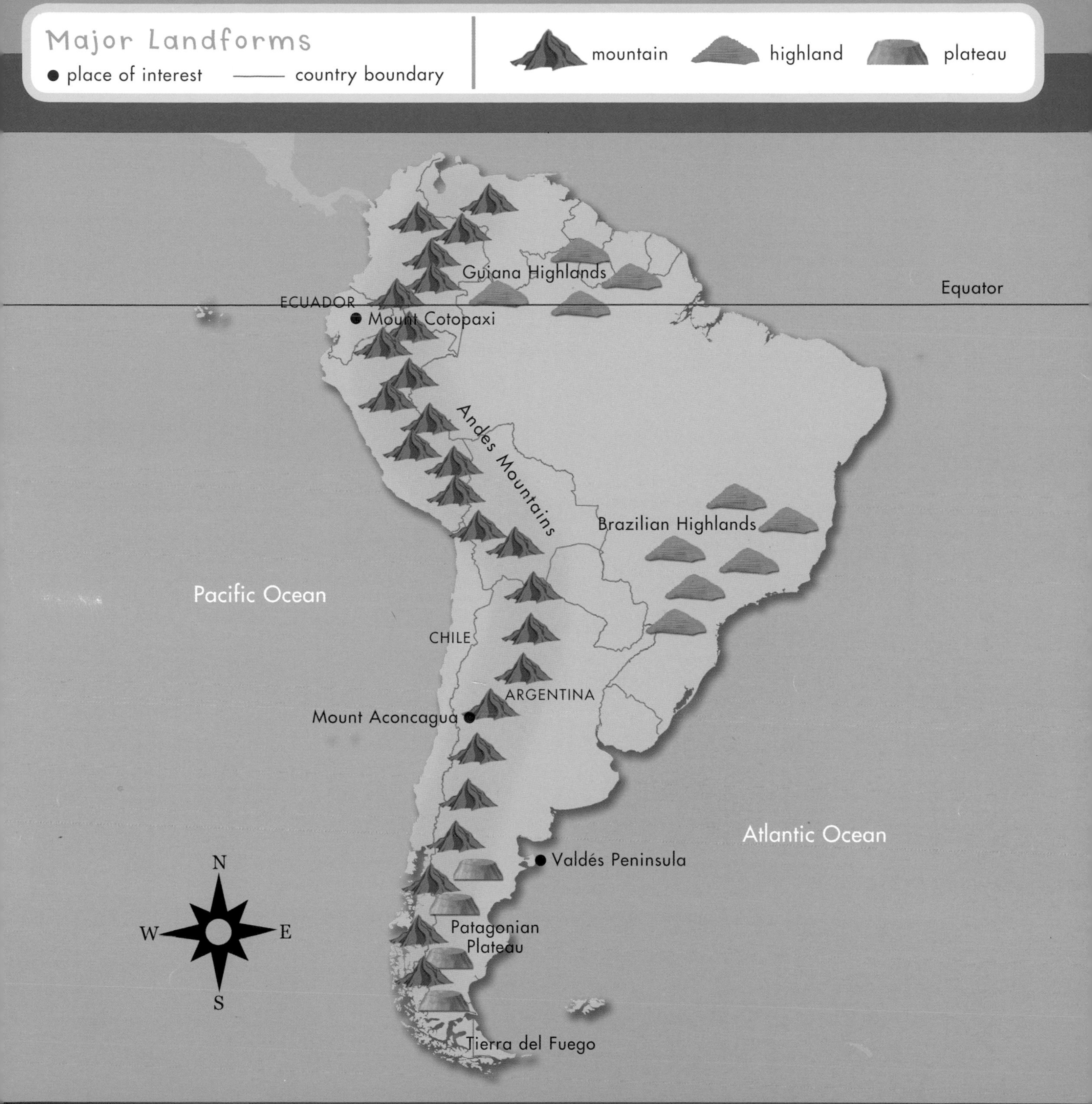

Equator

Guiana Highlands

ECUADOR
● Mount Cotopaxi

Andes Mountains

Brazilian Highlands

Pacific Ocean

CHILE

ARGENTINA

Mount Aconcagua ●

Atlantic Ocean

● Valdés Peninsula

N
W   E
S

Patagonian
Plateau

Tierra del Fuego

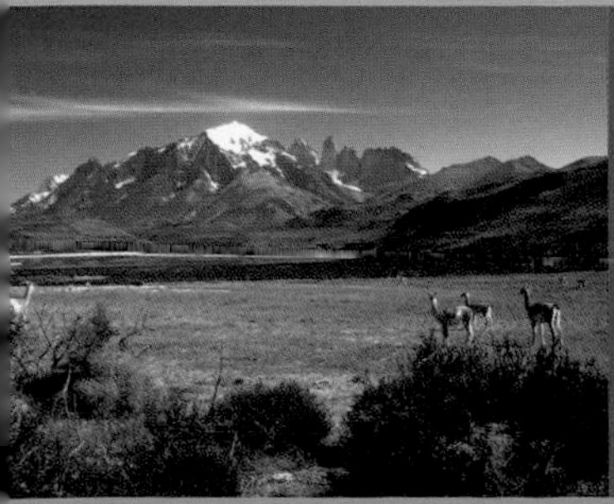

The Patagonian Plateau is a flat, dry, bare stretch of land in southern
Argentina. Some of the oldest rocks on Earth can be found there.

The Patagonian Plateau lies in the shadow of the Andes Mountains.

9

Bodies of Water

The Amazon River is the world's second-longest river. Apart from the main river, or branch, running from west to east, the Amazon has 1,000 tributaries. Tributaries are smaller rivers that feed larger ones.

The continent is also crisscrossed by many other large rivers. The Parana and Madeira rivers are the largest of these.

The Amazon River

The Amazon River starts as a small stream high in the Andes. It flows 4,000 miles (6,400 kilometers) across South America to the Atlantic Ocean. The Amazon carries more freshwater than any other river in the world.

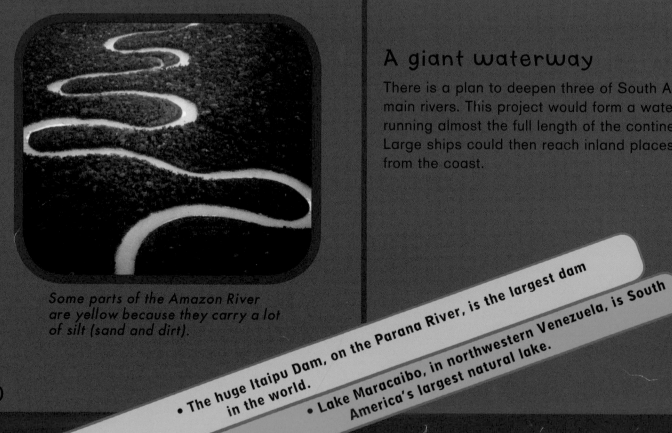

Some parts of the Amazon River are yellow because they carry a lot of silt (sand and dirt).

A "golden" lake

Lake Guatavita, in the mountains of Colombia, is believed to hold treasure. Legends tell how gold and gemstones were thrown into the water long ago by the Chibcha people. The treasures were gifts to their lake god, El Dorado, or "golden man." But the treasure has never been found.

Mighty women

In 1541, Spanish sailors exploring a river in South America were attacked by a group of native women. The women were very strong and fought hard. The Spaniards later named the river "Amazon," after a group of strong women fighters in a famous Greek legend.

A giant waterway

There is a plan to deepen three of South America's main rivers. This project would form a waterway running almost the full length of the continent. Large ships could then reach inland places far from the coast.

• The huge Itaipu Dam, on the Parana River, is the largest dam in the world.

• Lake Maracaibo, in northwestern Venezuela, is South America's largest natural lake.

Major Bodies of Water

● place of interest   ——— country boundary

⬠ lake   〰 river

Lake Maracaibo   VENEZUELA
Orinoco River

Lake Guatavita ●
COLOMBIA

● Angel Falls

Equator

Amazon River

Madeira River

PERU

Lake Titicaca

BOLIVIA

Parana River

● Itaipu
Dam

Pacific Ocean

ARGENTINA

Atlantic Ocean

N
W   E
S

Lake Titicaca is the world's highest lake that ships can sail on. It lies on the border between Bolivia and Peru.

Handwoven reed boats sail across the calm waters of Lake Titicaca.

In Venezuela, a tributary of the Orinoco River drops 3,212 feet (980 meters), forming the world's highest waterfall—Angel Falls.

Angel Falls

11

Much of South America has a tropical climate. Temperatures are hot all year. Rain is seasonal.

But some parts of the continent have dry, mild, or mountain climates. More than half of South America's countries have more than one climate.

Climate is the average weather a place has from season to season, year to year. Rainfall and temperature play large parts in a region's climate.

Seasonal rains

A tropical climate has two seasons: rainy and dry. During the dry season, land surrounding rivers may be covered with swampy forests. But during the wet season, when the rivers flood, the forests may disappear underwater.

Dry land

Parts of northern Chile haven't seen rain for 400 years! The few plants and animals that live there must get their water from mountain snow, fog, and dew.

Cloud forests

Cloud forests are common in the mountain climate of South America. These clouds form when hot air from the Pacific Ocean rises over the mountains and cools. The clouds are so low that the treetops rise above them.

Cloud forests are often seen along the western part of South America.

Climate basics

A region's climate depends upon three major things: how close it is to the ocean, how high up it is, and how close it is to the equator. Areas along the ocean have milder climates than areas farther inland. The higher a region is, and the farther it is from the equator, the colder its temperature.

- The largest desert in South America is the Patagonian. It is a cold desert. Most of the desert's precipitation (water) falls in the form of snow.
- Areas in South America with a tropical climate may receive more than 80 inches (2 meters) of rain each year.
- The Atacama Desert, in northern Chile, is the driest place on Earth.

Climate

| dry | dry most or all year with hot summers and warm to cold winters | mild | wet winters or all year with warm to hot summers and cool winters |

—— country boundary

| tropical | wet and dry seasons, hot all year | mountain | wet and dry seasons, cool to cold all year |

Equator

Pacific Ocean

Atacama Desert

CHILE

ARGENTINA

Atlantic Ocean

Patagonian Desert

N
W   E
S

Country of many climates

Chile has many different climates. The southern half of the country has a mild climate. The northern half has a dry climate. Regions along Chile's eastern border have a mountain climate.

Grapes grow well in Chile's mild climate.

13

Plants

Of South America's many ecosystems, the rain forest is the one most people think of first. An ecosystem is all of the living and nonliving things in a certain area. It includes plants, animals, soil, weather ... everything!

The Amazon Rain Forest is the largest rain forest in the world. It is more than one-third the size of the mainland United States! This amazing ecosystem is like a giant greenhouse, filled with countless trees, flowers, vines, and other plants.

Some Plants of South America

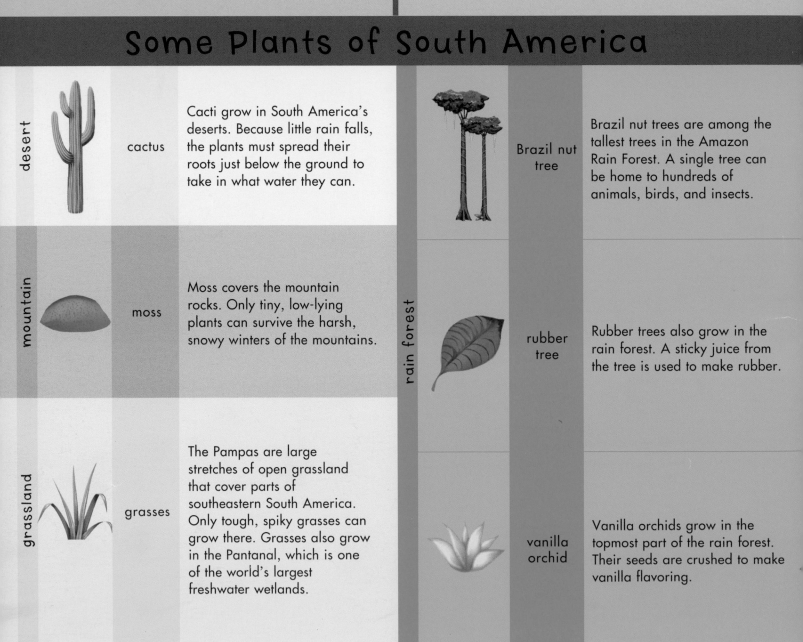

desert

cactus

Cacti grow in South America's deserts. Because little rain falls, the plants must spread their roots just below the ground to take in what water they can.

mountain

moss

Moss covers the mountain rocks. Only tiny, low-lying plants can survive the harsh, snowy winters of the mountains.

grassland

grasses

The Pampas are large stretches of open grassland that cover parts of southeastern South America. Only tough, spiky grasses can grow there. Grasses also grow in the Pantanal, which is one of the world's largest freshwater wetlands.

rain forest

Brazil nut tree

Brazil nut trees are among the tallest trees in the Amazon Rain Forest. A single tree can be home to hundreds of animals, birds, and insects.

rubber tree

Rubber trees also grow in the rain forest. A sticky juice from the tree is used to make rubber.

vanilla orchid

Vanilla orchids grow in the topmost part of the rain forest. Their seeds are crushed to make vanilla flavoring.

14

Major Ecosystems
—— country boundary

desert grassland rain forest wetlands
forest mountain tundra

Equator

Amazon
Rain Forest

Pantanal

Pacific Ocean

Atlantic Ocean

N
W E
S

Pampas

Patagonia

Animals

More than half of Earth's plant and animal species live in South America, especially in the Amazon Rain Forest. All are well-adapted to the ecosystems in which they live. An ecosystem is all of the living and nonliving things in a certain area.

Animals of South America include mammals such as monkeys, jaguars, and sloths; birds such as toucans, parrots, and owls; reptiles such as snakes, turtles, and lizards; many kinds of fish; and thousands and thousands of insect species.

Some Animals of South America

grassland	giant anteater	The giant anteater uses its narrow snout to suck ants and termites from their nests. Wild giant anteaters live in the grasslands and forests of Central and South America.
mountain	condor	The condor flies hundreds of miles each day, hunting for food.
mountain	llama	Llamas live in herds on the high mountain slopes.
rain forest	parrot	Parrots use bright feathers to find a mate in the dark forest.

	jaguar	The jaguar hunts small monkeys and birds in the jungle.
	piranha	Piranhas attack their prey with razor-sharp teeth. These fish are found in the Amazon and other freshwater rivers.
rain forest	blue morpho	The blue morpho butterfly is the size of a child's hand. This butterfly is found only in Central and South America.
	sloth	The sleepy sloth hangs upside down in the trees and hardly moves at all.
	toucan	The toucan is a fruit-eating bird with a huge, yellow bill.
	poison tree frog	The poison tree frog's bright red coloring warns enemies to stay away.

16

Major Ecosystems
—— country boundary

desert   grassland   rain forest   wetlands
forest   mountain   tundra

Equator

Amazon Rain Forest

Pacific Ocean

N
W   E
S

Atlantic Ocean

17

Population

Three-quarters of South America's population live in large, modern cities along the coast. There, bustling ports and harbors provide many people with jobs. Most of the continent's goods still arrive and leave by sea.

Farming the country

Only one-fourth of all South Americans live in the countryside. Most are poor and work on small farms. Life for these people has changed little over hundreds of years. In some places, small farms lie next to huge ranches owned by wealthy landowners.

Poor in the city

South America has a large number of people who are poor. Many of the poor live in shantytowns (*favelas*) built of wood, tin, and cardboard. The favelas on the hillsides of Rio de Janeiro are some of the best known.

Keeping with tradition

Native Americans make up more than half of Bolivia's population. Many still wear traditional ponchos, shawls, and round, felt hats.

Four big cities

The capital of Venezuela, **Caracas**, is one of the richest cities in South America. Most of the land around the city is used for mining and oil drilling.

Caracas, Venezuela

São Paulo, Brazil, has the largest population in South America. It borders a rich farming and industrial region.

The city of **Buenos Aires** lies on the coast of Argentina. Nearly 12 million people live there. It is the second-largest city on the continent.

Buenos Aires, Argentina

The Bolivian city of **La Paz** is one of the highest cities in the world. It is often called "the city that touches the clouds." La Paz is home to a large number of Native Americans.

• Few people, except Native Americans, live in the South American rain forests. It is too hot and humid.

• Because of the cold, oxygen-poor air, few people live in the high mountains.

18

People per Square Mile

- ● place of interest
- — country boundary

less than **5**	**5-25**	**25-125**	**125-250**	more than **250**

Caracas
VENEZUELA

Equator

BRAZIL

BOLIVIA
● La Paz

Pacific Ocean

São Paulo ● ● Rio de Janeiro

ARGENTINA

Buenos Aires

Atlantic Ocean

N
W E
S

In recent years, many people who once farmed in the mountains in northwestern South America have moved down to the coast to find better-paying jobs.

Farmland on a mountain slope in northwestern South America

DID YOU KNOW?

Brazil has a very young population. Almost half of the people who live there are under 20 years old.

19

People and Customs

South America is a mixture of many cultures and traditions. Parts of the continent were once ruled by Spain, Portugal, and France. Touches of these countries can still be seen in South America's art, food, religion, and music.

The traditions of Native Americans and people of African background continue to be strong parts of South America's rich culture, too.

Dressing up

Native Americans in the steamy forests of Brazil wear few clothes. Instead, they decorate themselves with jewelry made from stones and animal bones, teeth, claws, and feathers.

The mountain people of southern Peru wear colorful woolen shawls, cloaks, and blankets to keep warm.

Ecotourism

Ecotourism (nature tourism) is popular in South America because huge areas of land are still wild. Ecotourists come to see the continent's plants, animals, and landscapes.

An ecotourist in Chile

Marketplace

The marketplace is a colorful part of everyday life in South America. People come to buy and sell goods such as handwoven baskets and rugs, fruits, and vegetables. Many just come to meet their friends and catch up on local gossip.

A clothing stall in Bolivia

20

Learning for life

Native American schoolchildren in the Andes and the Amazon learn how to read and write. Most of them also learn life skills. For example, they may learn how to build and repair a house, how to make crafts, and how to grow food.

Children at a village school in the Andes

Yanomami village

The Yanomami people live in large, round, woven huts. They grow their own vegetables, hunt, and fish in the northern Amazon region. Until the early 1900s, the Yanomami had had no contact with anyone except other Native American groups.

Soccer mania

Soccer is very popular in Brazil. The former Brazilian player Pelé is said to be one of the greatest soccer players of all time. As a boy, Pelé was too poor to buy a soccer ball, so he played with a grapefruit stuffed in a sock! Today he is a national hero.

Festival of the Sun

Long ago, the Inca people of Peru worshipped the power of the sun. Today, a famous Peruvian festival honors the tradition. After watching the sun rise, people celebrate with music, food, and dance.

People celebrating the Festival of the Sun in Peru

21

Postcard Places

South America is full of interesting places—mountains, beaches, national parks and gardens, ancient ruins, and amazing modern cities.

Carnaval Time

Costumes, music, and dance are all parts of South America's annual Carnaval celebration.

Rising high above the bay, Sugar Loaf Mountain is the most famous landmark of Rio de Janeiro, Brazil.

Welcome to Rio

Amazon River

Chan Chan

Machu Picchu

Rio de Janeiro

Pampas

Easter Island

Decorative wall in the ancient city of Chan Chan

The city of Chan Chan, Peru, was built more than 1,000 years ago and was made entirely of mud.

Easter Island, off the coast of Chile, is best known for its giant stone statues, called the Moai.

Meet the Moai

Gauchos (cowboys) herd cattle on the grassy Pampas.

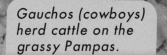

SADDLE UP!

Trek to Machu Picchu

Machu Picchu was an ancient city built in the Andes Mountains by a group of Native Americans called the Incas.

View from the Amazon River

Because the river often floods, houses on the banks of the Amazon are built on wooden stilts.

23

Growing and Making

South America is a continent with many natural resources.

Oil, metals, and gems are mined in the mountains and grasslands. Coffee, sugarcane, wheat, and other crops are grown. Cattle are raised. Fish are harvested from the surrounding oceans.

Most of these goods are exported, or shipped overseas.

Copper and emeralds

Many metals and gemstones lie within the mountains of western South America. Silver, gold, and copper are found there. The copper mines of Chile are the largest in the world. Emeralds are found in Colombia.

Emeralds are rare green gemstones. Here, they are being sorted by size and quality.

Drilling for oil

Venezuela's Lake Maracaibo is the largest lake in South America. Below the lake floor lie huge pockets of oil. Drills tap the oil, which is then pumped up into pipelines and carried all over the world.

An oil-drilling rig in Lake Maracaibo

Bananas

Even though Ecuador is the fourth-largest banana producer in the world, it exports more bananas than any other country.

- Coffee is grown on tree farms. The beans are picked in the dry season, when they're bright red, then dried and roasted. Brazil and Colombia are the top coffee producers in the world.
- Sugarcane is a kind of tall grass. The sugar is found in the stalks. Brazil produces most of the world's sugar.

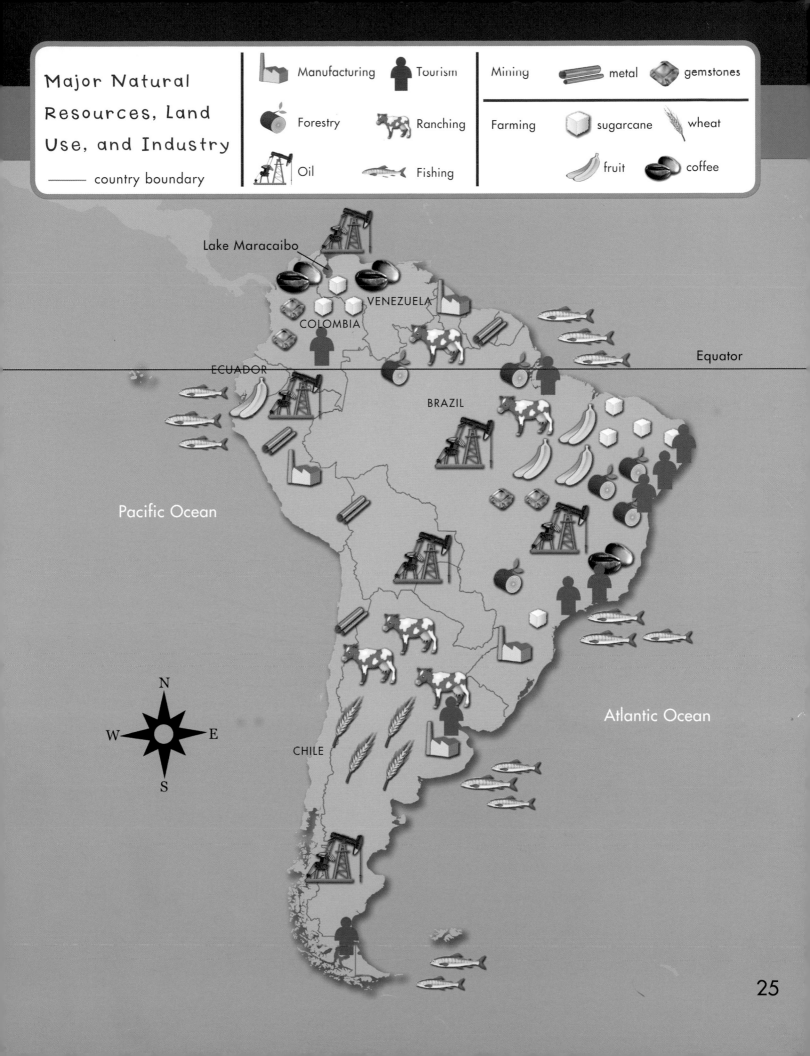

Major Natural Resources, Land Use, and Industry

Manufacturing   Tourism

Forestry   Ranching

Oil   Fishing

Mining   metal   gemstones

Farming   sugarcane   wheat

fruit   coffee

—— country boundary

Lake Maracaibo

VENEZUELA

COLOMBIA

ECUADOR

Equator

BRAZIL

Pacific Ocean

CHILE

Atlantic Ocean

N
W   E
S

Transportation

Moving people and goods by land in South America is difficult because of the towering mountains and the thick jungles.

However, air travel is now quick and easy. A growing number of railways and bus routes also connect parts of the continent.

Waterways are one of the most common ways to transport people and goods in South America.

Riding the rails

South America doesn't have a well-developed major railway system. But many countries have their own local systems.

To travel through the mountains, most South Americans either walk or use the trains.

Dugout canoes

For the Amazon's river people, canoes are the easiest way of getting around. Fishermen haul their catch up and down the river. Others trade tools and crafts for food as they travel from village to village.

A dugout canoe carries people downriver.

Friendship Bridge

The Ponte da Amizade, or Friendship Bridge, connects Paraguay to Brazil. Most goods are carried in and out of Paraguay over the bridge.

Rough roads

Good roads outside of South America's big cities are rare. Many country roads are steep mountain paths or rough tracks. They are often carved out over time by llamas or heavy-wheeled carts and wagons.

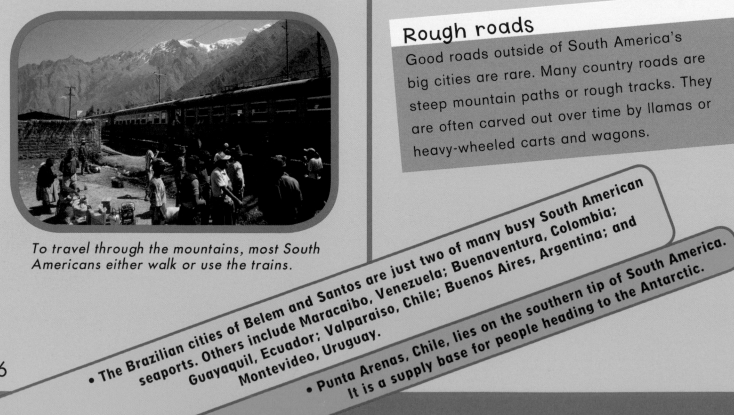

- The Brazilian cities of Belem and Santos are just two of many busy South American seaports. Others include Maracaibo, Venezuela; Buenaventura, Colombia; Guayaquil, Ecuador; Valparaiso, Chile; Buenos Aires, Argentina; and Montevideo, Uruguay.
- Punta Arenas, Chile, lies on the southern tip of South America. It is a supply base for people heading to the Antarctic.

Major Transportation Routes

● place of interest —— country boundary

━━ major highway ━━ major waterway

Maracaibo●
Lake Maracaibo VENEZUELA
Orinoco River
Buenaventura● COLOMBIA
Equator
ECUADOR
Guayaquil● Negro River Manaus Obidos● Belem●
Amazon River Central Amazon Highway
BRAZIL
Pan American Highway
Lake Titicaca Paraguay River São Francisco River
Parana River
Pacific Ocean
PARAGUAY
Santos●
Ponte da Amizade (Friendship Bridge)
CHILE
ARGENTINA
URUGUAY
Valparaiso● Montevideo●
Buenos Aires●
Atlantic Ocean

N
W E
S

Punta Arenas●

Boats travel up and down the Amazon River, stopping at Manaus and Obidos, Brazil, and other river ports along the way.

Llamas are important to the people of the mountains. The animals carry loads along steep, narrow paths.

27

Journey Around Lake Titicaca

The train to Lake Titicaca climbs up and up. All around are the low foothills of the Andes Mountains. Steep, snow-capped mountain peaks rise in the distance.

The passengers on this train are on their way to celebrate the legend of Manco Capac and his sister. The two were honored as the children of the sun, a god who rose from the waters of Lake Titicaca and started the Inca empire.

Lake Titicaca

More than 25 rivers empty into Lake Titicaca. The huge lake covers more than 3,200 square miles (8,320 square kilometers). It is the highest lake in the world that can be crossed by boat.

At the celebration, passengers will dance, listen to music, and feast on grilled catfish and trout.

Passengers look out their windows at the 41 islands on Lake Titicaca. Families plant wheat, potatoes, and other vegetables on the islands. They also raise cattle, sheep, and alpacas for their meat, milk, and wool.

Huge rafts called totoras float in the shallow water around the lake. The Uros people weave these rafts, their huts, boats, and crafts from reeds that grow in the lake.

Once the train stops, passengers will be able to watch the local people weaving and then buy some souvenirs.

Weaving a totora reed boat

South America At-a-Glance

Continent size: the fourth-largest of Earth's seven continents

Number of countries: 13

Major languages:
- Spanish
- Portuguese
- English
- French
- Native American languages

Total population: 371 million (2005 estimate)

Largest country (land size): Brazil

Most populated country: Brazil

Most populated city: São Paulo, Brazil

Climate: humid, tropical climate along the equator; mild in the Southeast and along the southwestern coast; dry in the South with hot summers and warm to cold winters; cool to cold in the mountains

Highest point: Mount Aconcagua, Argentina, 22,834 feet (6,964 meters)

Lowest point: Valdés Peninsula, Argentina, 132 feet (40 m) below sea level

Longest river: Amazon River

Largest body of water: Lake Maracaibo

Largest desert: Patagonian Desert

Major agricultural products:
- bananas
- beef
- cocoa beans
- coffee
- corn
- cotton
- cut flowers
- dairy products
- grapes
- rice
- soybeans
- sugarcane
- wheat

Major industries:
- fishing
- lumber
- oil
- manufacturing (consumer goods such as clothing, beverages, motor vehicles, electrical and mechanical equipment, and plastics)

Natural resources:
- bauxite
- copper
- gemstones
- iron
- lead
- manganese
- natural gas
- oil
- tin
- zinc

Glossary

body of water – a mass of water that is in one area; such as a river, lake, or ocean

boundary – a line that shows the border of a country, state, or other land area

climate – the average weather a place has from season to season, year to year

compass rose – a symbol used to show direction on a map

continent – one of seven large land masses on Earth, including Africa, Antarctica, Asia, Australia, Europe, North America, and South America

crops – plants that are grown in large amounts and are used for food or income

desert – a hot or cold, very dry area that has few plants growing on it

ecosystem – all of the living and nonliving things in a certain area, including plants, animals, soil, and weather

equator – an imaginary line around Earth; it divides the northern and southern hemispheres

forest – land covered by trees and plants

forestry – the work of growing and caring for forests

grassland – land covered mostly with grass

harbor – a sheltered place along a coast

highland – high or hilly land

island – land that is completely surrounded by water

lake – a body of water that is completely surrounded by land

landform – a natural feature on Earth's surface

legend – the part of a map that explains the meaning of the map's symbols

mountain – a mass of land that rises high above the land that surrounds it

natural resources – materials such as water, trees, and minerals that are found in nature

North Pole – the northern-most point on Earth

ocean – the large body of saltwater that covers most of Earth's surface

peninsula – a body of land that is surrounded by water on three sides

plateau – a large, flat, and often rocky area of land that is higher than the surrounding land

population – the total number of people who live in one area

port – a place where ships can load or unload cargo (goods or people)

rain forest – a thick forest that receives a lot of rain year-round

ranching – the work of raising animals such as cattle and sheep on a ranch

river – a large stream of water that empties into a lake, ocean, or other river

scale – the size of a map or model compared to the actual size of things they stand for

South Pole – the southern-most point on Earth

species – groups of animals or plants that have many things in common

temperature – how hot or cold something is

tributary – a stream or river that flows into a larger river

tundra – land with no trees that lies in the arctic regions

valley – a low place between mountains or hills

wetland – an area that has very wet soil and is covered with water at least part of the year

Index

animals, 12, 16, 23, 24, 25, 27
Antarctic Circle, 4–5
Arctic Circle, 4–5
Argentina, 7, 9, 18, 26
art, 20

Brazil, 6
Bolivia, 6, 7, 18

Chile, 7, 12, 13, 23, 24, 26
cities, 18, 23, 26
climate, 12, 13
clothing, 20
cloud forests, 12
Colombia, 6, 7, 24
compass rose, 4
continents, 4–5
countries, 6, 7

dancing, 6, 29
dry climate, 13
dry season, 12

ecotourism, 20
ecosystems, 14, 15, 16, 17, 20
Ecuador, 6, 7, 8, 25, 26
education, 21
equator, 4–5, 12
exports, 24

farming, 18, 19, 23, 24, 25, 29
festivals, 6, 21, 22
food, 6, 20, 29
forests, 12, 14, 16
French Guiana, 7

gorges, 8

Guyana, 6, 7

highlands, 8

islands, 8, 23, 29
Isthmus of Panama, 4, 5

lakes, 10, 11, 28–29
languages, 6
legend, 4
lowlands, 8

marketplaces, 20
mild climate, 12, 13
mining, 24
mountain climate, 12, 13
mountains, 8, 12, 13, 22
music, 20, 29

Native Americans, 6, 18, 20, 21, 23, 26
natural resources, 24, 25

Paraguay, 6, 7, 26
people, 6, 18, 19, 20–21, 23, 26
Peru, 21, 22
plants, 12, 14, 16
plateaus, 8, 9
population, 18, 19

rain forests, 14, 16
rainy season, 12
religion, 20
rivers, 10, 11, 12, 23, 26, 27

scale bar, 5
shantytowns, 18

sports, 21
Suriname, 7

transportation, 10, 11, 26, 27, 28, 29
tributaries, 10, 11
Tropic of Cancer, 5
Tropic of Capricorn, 5
tropical climate, 13

Uruguay, 7, 26

Venezuela, 7, 11, 18, 24, 26
volcanoes, 8

On the Web

FactHound offers a safe, fun way to find Web sites related to topics in this book.
All of the sites on FactHound have been researched by our staff.

1. Visit *www.facthound.com*
2. Type in this special code: 1404838872
3. Click on the FETCH IT button.

Your trusty FactHound will fetch the best sites for you!

Look for all of the books in the Picture Window Books
World Atlases series:

Atlas of Africa
Atlas of Australia
Atlas of Europe
Atlas of North America
Atlas of South America
Atlas of Southwest and Central Asia
Atlas of the Far East and Southeast Asia
Atlas of the Poles and Oceans